Life begins at

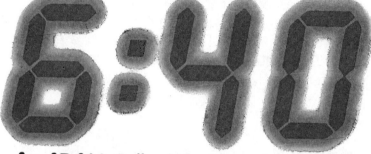

An ADAM Collection by Brian Basset

Andrews and McMeel
A Universal Press Syndicate Company
Kansas City

For Keegan and Trevor.

Keep doodling.

But not necessarily on each other.

Love,

Dad

7

11

13

29

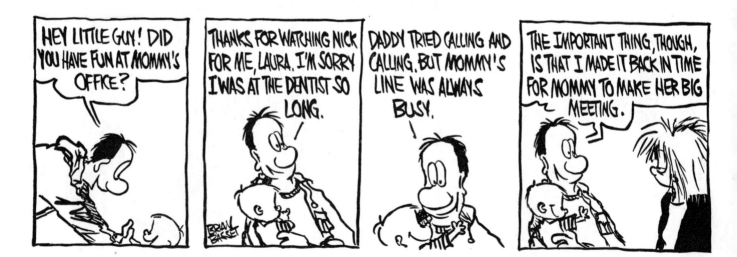

Row 1:

POOR ADAM'S GOING THROUGH A REAL SELF-IMAGE PROBLEM RIGHT NOW.

OVER STAYING AT HOME?

NO, THAT WAS LAST MONTH, THIS TIME IT'S HIS HAIR... OR LACK OF IT.

DOES THAT BOTHER YOU?

NO!

THEN TELL HIM THAT! TELL HIM IT'S NO BIG DEAL. TELL HIM HE'S THE SEXIEST MAN ALIVE.

LIKE A KEVIN COSTNER WITHOUT HAIR.

WHAT A HORRIBLE THOUGHT!

Row 2:

D'YA THINK ADAM WOULD EVER WEAR A HAIRPIECE?

NAH, AS MUCH AS HE DOESN'T LIKE LOSING HIS HAIR, HE'S A "NATURAL" KIND OF A GUY.

HOW 'BOUT A HAIR TRANSPLANT THEN?

TOO PAINFUL.

NO, EVEN THOUGH HIS VANITY IS GETTING THE BEST OF HIM RIGHT NOW, I DON'T SEE THIS AS BEING A REAL PROBLEM FOR ADAM.

MAYBE, JUST MAYBE, I COULD GROW THE HAIRS ON MY BACK AND SHOULDERS REAL LONG AND COMB THEM UP AND OVER MY HEAD.

BRIAN BASSET

Row 3:

MY, YOU SEEM CHIPPER THIS MORNING.

THAT'S BECAUSE I'VE BEEN READING ABOUT ALL THE HORRIBLE THINGS THAT ARE HAPPENING IN THE WORLD RIGHT NOW!

WHILE I'VE BEEN SELFISHLY CONCERNED OVER LOSING A FEW DUMB STRANDS OF HAIR, OTHERS ARE BEING HIT BY TRAGEDIES OF ENORMOUS PROPORTIONS.

SURE. MAKES PERFECT SENSE TO ME.

YUP! TODAY'S LOOKING UP!

BRIAN BASSET

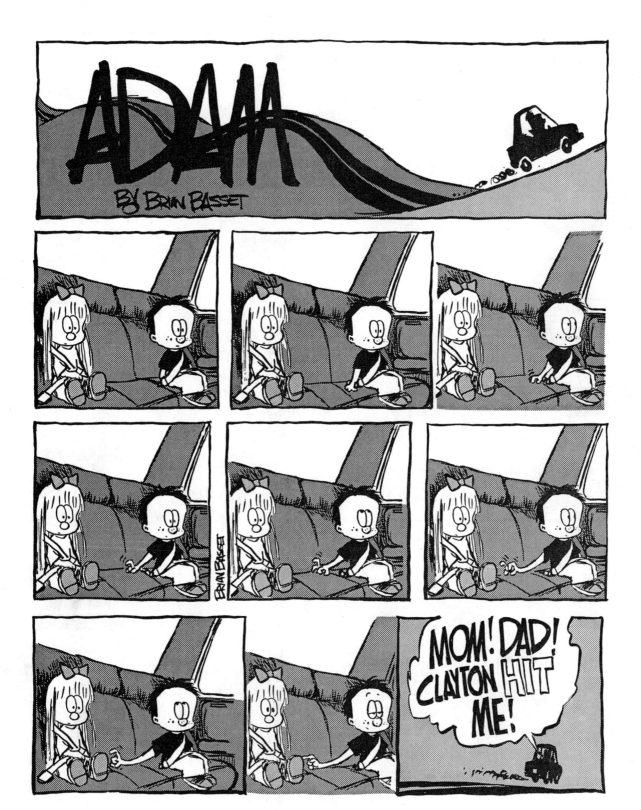

41

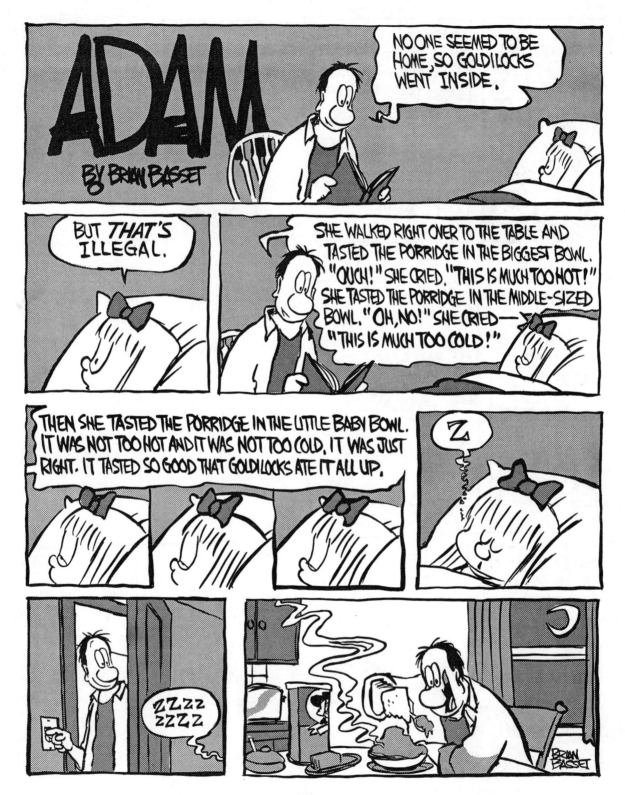

47

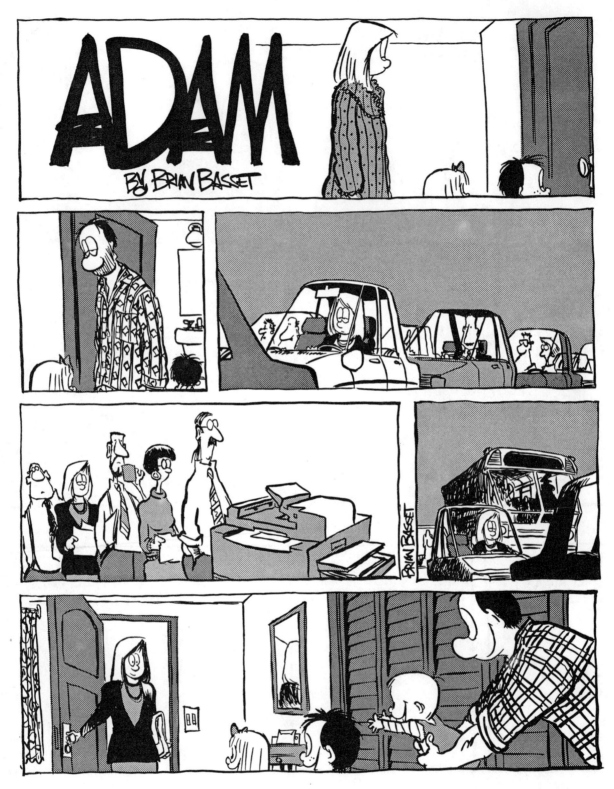

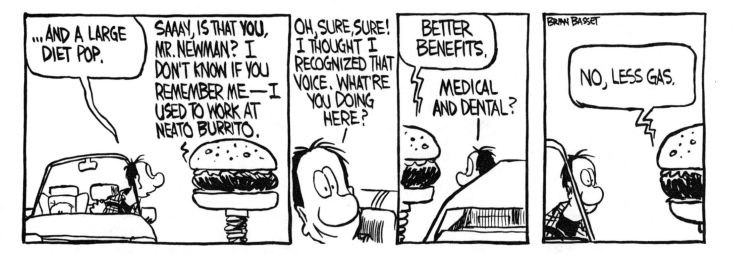

COMPUTER VIRUS

The real cause of GLOBAL WARMING

BUT DAAAAD. ALL MY FRIENDS HAVE NINTENDO!

SEE— YOU DON'T NEED TO GET ONE THEN. YOU CAN JUST PLAY IT OVER AT THEIR HOUSES.

WELL,,, IT WON'T BE MY FAULT THAT I DON'T GET INTO THE COLLEGE OF MY CHOICE BECAUSE I DIDN'T LOG ENOUGH HOURS BEHIND THE VIDEO SCREEN!

COLLEGE OF YOUR CHOICE??

YEAH— STARFLEET ACADEMY.

Dear Santa.

This past year I have been especially good, and would like a Nintendo set for Christmas.

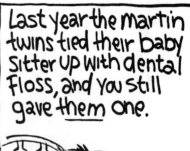

Last year the martin twins tied their baby sitter up with dental floss, and you still gave them one.

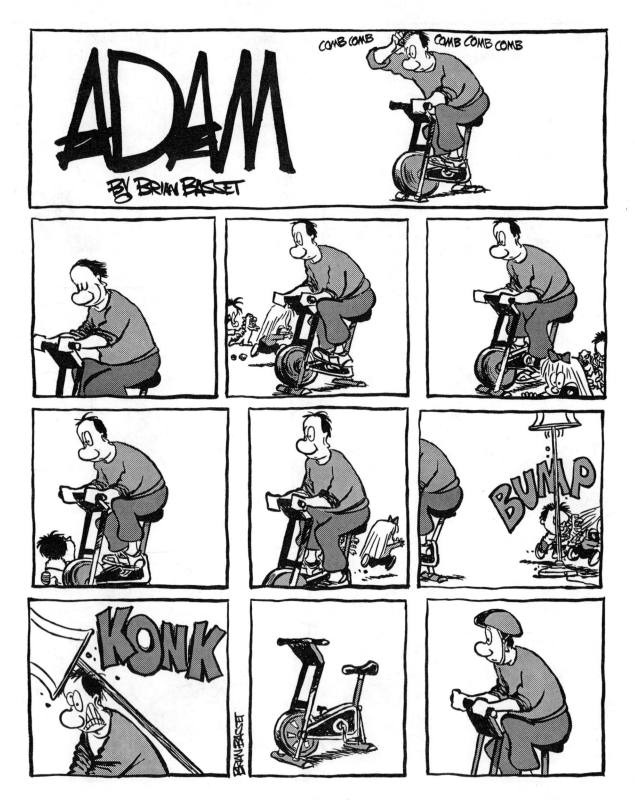

87

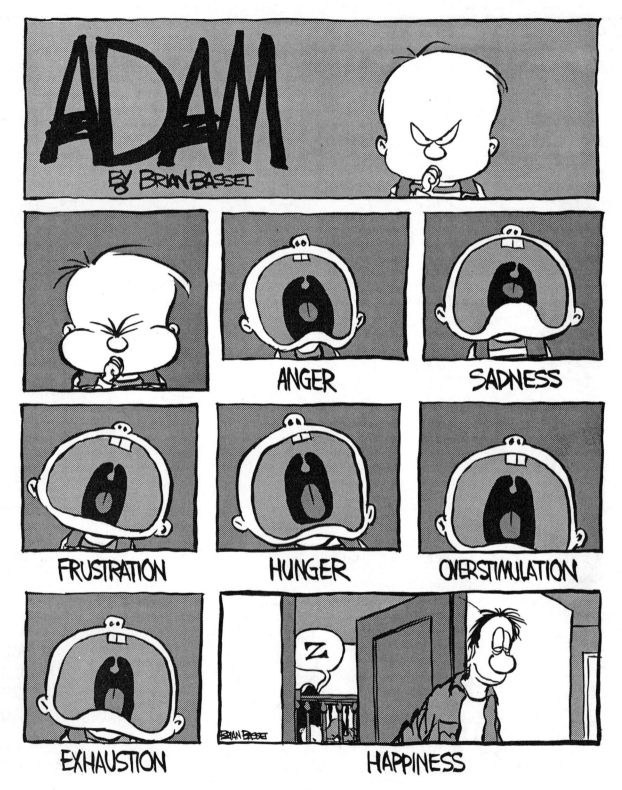

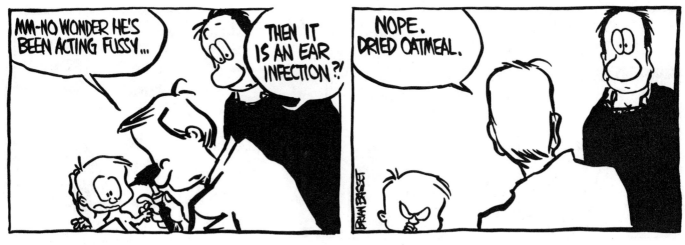

ADAM. THE BABY'S CRYING AGAIN.

KATY. YOUR TOOTH PROBABLY HURTS BECAUSE YOU JUST HAD COLD ICE CREAM. BELIEVE ME. A BANDAID ON YOUR TOOTH WON'T DO ANY GOOD.

YES IT WILL! I NEED A BAND-AID!!

I NEED A BAND-AID! I NEED A BAND-AID! I NEED A BAND-AID! I NEED A...

LUCKY FOR YOU WE HAD ONE NINJA TURTLE BAND-AID LEFT. NOW HOLD STILL.

THERE! THAT SHOULD MAKE YOUR TOOTH HEAL FASTER THAN THAT NEON BATMAN GLOW-IN-THE-DARK BAND-AID YOU HAD ON BEFORE.

HEY! MY OOTH EELS ETTER ALL EDDY!!

AND IT'S LESS NOTICEABLE, TOO!

HERE! SEE HOW THE GREEN TURTLE COLOR OF THE BAND-AID RESEMBLES CHEWED-UP FOOD!

PAINTING EASTER EGGS, WHY?

...AND A FEW STROKES FOR THE WHISKERS... AND *VOILA!*... A LONG-EARED GOOFY BUNNY RABBIT!

HOW'S THIS? I WAS ONLY ABLE TO FIT HALF OF MICHELANGELO'S SISTINE CHAPEL ON MY EGG.

AND I'M ALMOST DONE PAINTING THE MAP OF THE WORLD ON MINE. BUT I DON'T THINK I GOT ALL THE NEW INDEPENDENT STATES RIGHT.

DID YOU REMEMBER TO HIDE THE KIDS' EASTER CANDY?

UH-HUH.

I PUT IT ON THE FLOOR IN THEIR ROOMS UNDERNEATH A PILE OF CLOTHES SCATTERED ABOUT.

THEY'LL *NEVER* LOOK THERE.

99

THE END